‹MADAGASCAR›

MAJOR WORLD NATIONS

MADAGASCAR

Rita Stevens

CHELSEA HOUSE PUBLISHERS
Philadelphia

Chelsea House Publishers
Contributing Author: Joseph Barron

Copyright © 1999 by Chelsea House Publishers,
a division of Main Line Book Co.
All rights reserved.
Printed and bound in the United States of America.

First Printing

1   3   5   7   9   8   6   4   2

Library of Congress Cataloging-in-Publication Data

Stevens, Rita.
Madagascar.
Includes index.

Summary: Presents an overview of the geography, history, economy,
culture, and people of this island country.

1. Madagascar. [1. Madagascar]
I. Title.
DT469.M26S94   1987   969'.1   87-11624

ISBN 0-7910-4762-8

‹CONTENTS›

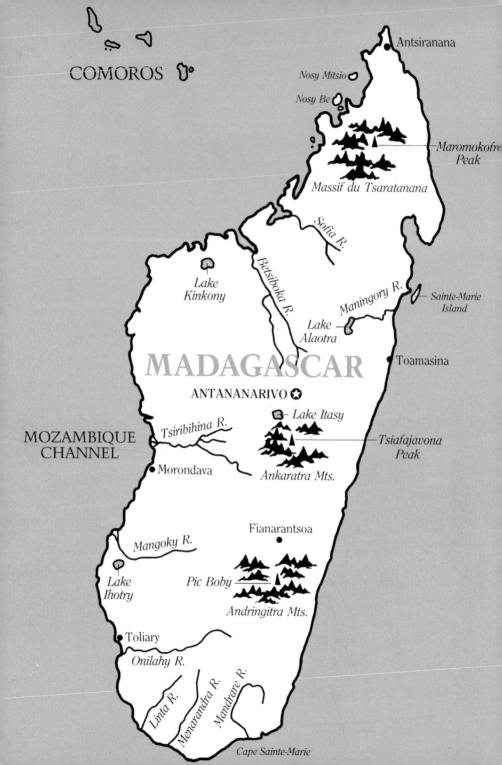

INDIAN OCEAN

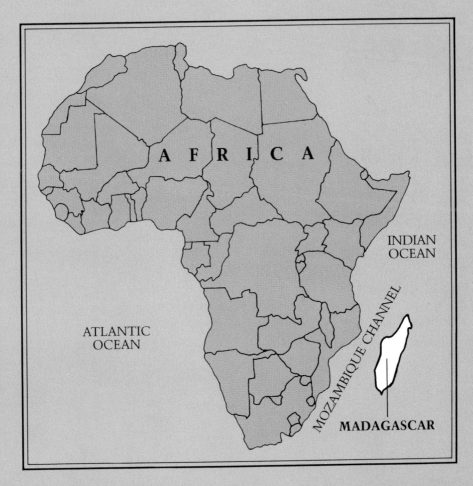

INDIAN
OCEAN

ATLANTIC
OCEAN

MOZAMBIQUE CHANNEL

MADAGASCAR

◄ FACTS AT A GLANCE ►

Land and People

Area	226,658 square miles (587,040 square kilometers)
Highest Point	Maromokofro Peak, 9,436 feet (2,876 meters)
Greatest Length	976 miles (1,571 km)
Greatest Width	335 miles (539 km)
Major Rivers	Mandrare, Menarandra, Linta, Sofia, Onilahy
Major Lakes	Itasy, Aloatra, Ihotry, Kinkony
Capital	Antananarivo (population 1 million)
Other Major Cities	Toamasina (population 200,000), Fianarantsoa (population 150,000)
Population	14 million
Population Density	62 people per square mile (24 per square km)
Population Distribution	Rural, 78 percent; urban, 22 percent
Official Languages	Malagasy, French
Literacy Rate	80 percent
Ethnic Groups	Merina, 26 percent; Betsimisaraka, 15 percent; Betsileo, 12 percent; Tsimihety, 7 percent; Sakalava, 6 percent; Antandroy, 5 percent; 11 other Malagasy clans, 28 percent; a few French, Asians, and Comoran Islanders
Religions	Traditional beliefs, 55 percent; Christian, 40 percent; Muslim, 5 percent

Infant Mortality Rate	94 per 1,000 live births
Average Life Expectancy	51 years for males; 53 for females

Economy

Chief Products	Vanilla, coffee, cloves, sugarcane, rice, shellfish, processed foods, textiles
Natural Resources	Graphite, chromite, coal, bauxite, ilmenite, tar sands, semiprecious stones, hardwood
Labor Force	4.9 million; 88 percent employed in subsistence agriculture; other nonwage workers, 8 percent; wage earners, 4 percent
Land Use	Meadows and pastures, 58 percent; arable, 4 percent; forest, 26 percent; other, 11 percent
Currency	Franc, divided into 100 centimes
Gross Domestic Product	$11.4 billion (1995), $820 per capita

Government

Form of Government	Multi-party republic
Formal Head of State	President, elected to a five-year term
Head of Government	Prime Minister, appointed by the president
Legislature	National Assembly, composed of 138 members
Local Government	Six provinces, divided into districts, village council assemblies, and villages

◄HISTORY AT A GLANCE►

about 400 A.D.	Madagascar's first inhabitants migrate from Malaysia and Indonesia. Other settlers, including a few Africans and Arabs, arrive in the following centuries.
by 900	Much of Madagascar is inhabited. Arab traders begin making visits to the island.
1500	Diogo Dias, a Portuguese navigator, is the first European known to have landed on Madagascar.
1500s	The Portuguese land on the island to raid the villages for food and women. They call it the Isle of St. Lawrence. By the end of the century, the Portuguese have failed to drive the Arabs out of their trading settlements on the north shore.
1643 to 1674	The French maintain a colony at Fort Dauphin on the southeast coast.
late 1600s and early 1700s	France colonizes the nearby Mascarene and Comoros island groups. Madagascar becomes a haunt of pirates, including the idealistic French pirate Misson.
1697	William Kidd, a notorious pirate captain, visits Misson's pirate settlement in northern Madagascar.
1700s	The Merina kingdom rises to prominence in the central highlands. Four chiefs vie for power.
1797	King Andrianampoinimerina is the first ruler to unite the Merina under a single leader.

1810 to 1828	King Radama I forms an alliance with the British and brings the entire island under Merina control.
1828 to 1861	Queen Ranavalona the Terrible outlaws Christianity and isolates Madagascar from European influence. Her troops defeat a combined British and French attack in 1845.
1861 to 1863	King Radama II allows the British and French to set up trade centers and churches on the island.
1863	General Rainilaiarivony seizes power and marries the next three Merina queens one after the other. He patterns the state religion and the government on European models.
1883 to 1885	The French give money and weapons to the Sakalava tribes of the southwest to fight against the Merina.
1890	Great Britain allows France to claim the island as a protectorate. The Merina refuse to submit to French rule.
1895	French troops take control of the island and exile Rainilaiarivony and Queen Ranavalona III to Algeria.
1896	Madagascar formally becomes a French colony. General Joseph Gallieni, the first governor-general, stamps out all resistance to French rule by 1905.
1905 to 1945	Madagascar's cities grow and its economy gains some strength. A secret society called the Vy Vato Sakelika (VVS) leads protests against French rule.
1945	As a result of support for the Free French movement during World War II, Madagascar is allowed to send representatives to the French Parliament.

1946   The island becomes an overseas territory of France.

1947   A nationalist organization leads an unsuccessful rebellion against the French.

1956   Philibert Tsiranana forms the Social Democratic party and promotes cooperation among the Merina and the other Malagasy peoples.

1958   The Malagasy vote to become self-governing members of the French Community. The Malagasy Republic is declared. Tsiranana is elected president.

1960   The republic becomes completely independent.

1972   Tsiranana resigns. Gabriel Ramanantsoa becomes prime minister. The island experiences extreme unrest.

1975   Martial law is declared. The armed forces turn the government over to Didier Ratsiraka. He dissolves the Malagasy Republic and sets up the Democratic Republic of Madagascar.

1975 to 1990   Ratsiraka attempts to establish government control over the economy, but later institutes free-market reforms. His authoritarian rule prompts increasing opposition.

1991   A general strike begins. The Presidential Guard kills more than 30 protesters at a mass antigovernment rally. Ratsiraka agrees to a transition to democracy.

1992   A new constitution is approved in a national referendum. Open presidential elections are held in November.

1993   Opposition leader Albert Zafy is elected president in a runoff election. In parliamentary elections, a coalition of parties allied to Zafy wins a majority in the National Assembly.

1996   Zafy is impeached by the parliament for attempting to dismiss the prime minister. An emergency election is held; Ratsiraka is declared the winner.

Isolated from the rest of the world, Madagascar developed into a land of exotic plants and animals. In about 400 A.D., it became home to the Malagasy people.

Madagascar and the World

For many years, the island of Madagascar in the Indian Ocean was a historical and geographical puzzle. On the map, it seems very close to Africa. The Mozambique Channel, which separates it from the African continent, is only 500 miles (805 kilometers) wide, leading many people to think of Madagascar as an African country. Despite Madagascar's political and trade relationships with African nations, however, its people and culture are not African at all. Its native inhabitants are the Malagasy (pronounced mah-lah-GAH-shee), who originated in Malaysia and Indonesia and reached Madagascar about 1,500 years ago. The Malagasy are quite different from their African neighbors. Their language, customs, and physical appearance reflect their Asian ancestry.

The origin of the Malagasy mystified geographers for centuries. The Western World first became aware of them and their island through the writings of Marco Polo, the Italian traveler who visited China and other parts of Asia in the 13th century. Although he never visited Madagascar, Polo had heard tales of the island—which he called Mogadishu—from Arab traders and merchants. He thought the island's inhabitants were Islamic Arabs, a belief that later was proved wrong. In a book narrating his travels, which he wrote in

1298 while he was jailed in Genoa as a political prisoner, he said of Mogadishu: "You must know that this island is one of the biggest and best in the whole world."

Many people ridiculed Marco Polo's tales, labeling them wild inventions; most were certain that Madagascar did not even exist. But when Europeans began to explore the Indian Ocean islands in the 16th century, they discovered that the great island did indeed exist. Soon, the Portuguese and French sent many expeditions to Madagascar, hoping to discover gold or jewels.

Few people believed 13th-century explorer Marco Polo when he wrote about Madagascar's wonders.

Although they found little treasure, those who explored the islands brought back reports of a strange land filled with man-eating trees, birds larger than horses, rivers of blood, and other natural marvels. They also returned with tales of the island's people, whom they mistakenly believed were Africans.

During the 18th and 19th centuries, Great Britain and France sent missionaries and traders to Madagascar. The two nations competed with each other to win converts to Christianity and to obtain favorable trade agreements from the Malagasy kings and queens who then ruled the island. During this period, scholars discovered that the island's native inhabitants were not of African origin. At the end of the 19th century, geographers and historians finally agreed that the Malagasy were related to the Indonesian and Polynesian peoples of Southeast Asia and the Pacific Islands.

In the 18th and 19th centuries, as European nations hurried to colonize the distant shores of Africa, Asia, and South America, France began to influence Madagascar. The French took official control of the island in 1896 and retained possession of Madagascar for half a century. But after World War II, most African colonies formed strong nationalistic movements (movements based on the belief that they should be free to govern themselves). Colonies began moving toward independence—some violently, some more slowly and peacefully.

During this period, riots and political demonstrations shook Madagascar. As a result, France allowed the colony to form its own government in 1958. The island became the Malagasy Republic and held its first elections. In 1960, France granted the island complete independence.

Unlike some other colonies, the Malagasy Republic retained close ties with the West after it gained independence. France, Great Britain, and the United States became the republic's biggest trading partners and sponsored programs to increase food production and

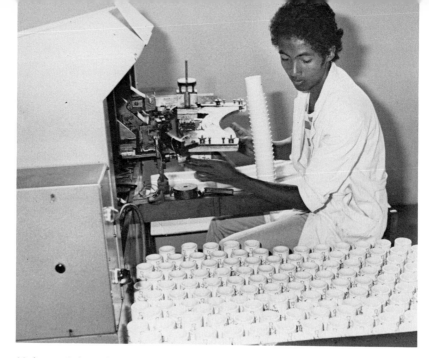

Madagascar's few industries include a yogurt-packing plant in Antananarivo.

improve health care. Although Malagasy became the islanders' official language, many continued to speak French. Virtually all aspects of Malagasy society—from law codes to food preparation—continued to reflect a strong French influence.

Between 1972 and 1975, uprisings and riots again rocked the island. This time, students and young workers protested food and job shortages and the presence of prosperous foreigners in the country. The rioters destroyed property, and some lost their lives. The government was unable to restore order, and in 1975 the army took control of the country. The military leaders dissolved the Malagasy Republic and created the Democratic Republic of Madagascar.

The new regime immediately launched a Socialist economic program, nationalizing sectors of the economy previously controlled by the French. Its policies produced no material benefits, however. As early as 1977, demonstrations erupted in response to severe shortages of food and other essential commodities. The government resorted to authoritarian tactics to maintain order, but succeeded only in fueling opposition.

By the early 1990s, continuing mass protests and the deteriorating economic situation forced the government to agree to fundamental changes. Free-market economic reforms were instituted. In 1992, a new constitution was approved by referendum, and the next year a democratically elected president and National Assembly came to power.

Today, Madagascar remains poor and depends on outside aid to keep the government and economy functioning. The island has potentially valuable natural resources, but lacks the modern industries necessary to make them profitable. Only four percent of the labor force work for monetary wages; the vast majority eke out their living in subsistence agriculture.

Madagascar quarreled with the United States during the 1970s, when it closed a U.S.-operated satellite tracking station and expelled the U.S. ambassador on two occasions. The situation began to improve in 1980, however, when diplomatic relations resumed. In 1990, the United States designated Madagascar as a priority aid recipient; each year, it grants tens of millions of dollars in aid for family planning programs, development of the private sector and democratic institutions, environmental protection, and agriculture.

Madagascar is a fascinating land. Many of its exotic plants and animals are found nowhere else on earth. Its unique culture includes such diverse elements as age-old magic rituals and modern motorscooters. Its political and economic development are poised between the old and the new, East and West. It remains to be seen in what direction Madagascar will move in the years ahead. Whatever happens, the island's future will undoubtedly be influenced by its physical attributes, its culture, and its past.

The Great Red Island's central plateau is an area of rugged, mountainous terrain. Although some hills are forested, most are bare mounds of laterite.

The Great Red Island

The largest of the Indian Ocean's many islands, Madagascar is the fourth largest island in the world (after Greenland, New Guinea, and Borneo). It covers an area of 226,658 square miles (587,040 square kilometers), about the size of the states of Pennsylvania, Ohio, Indiana, Illinois, and Iowa combined. The island is shaped like an irregular oval, 976 miles (1,571 kilometers) long and 335 miles (539 km) across at its widest point. It is composed almost entirely of laterite, a type of stone that crumbles into reddish soil. Although dense, dark green forests and lighter green rice fields cover parts of the island, most of it consists of bare, red earth rising steeply from the sea. Madagascar's distinctive color has led its inhabitants and the people of neighboring lands to call it "The Great Red Island."

Madagascar is divided into three regions that run north and south along the length of the island. One region consists of a narrow strip of tropical lowland along the eastern coast, which is bordered by the Indian Ocean. A high, mountainous central plateau comprises another region. The third region, the western part of the island, is characterized by broad, hilly plains.

The island's eastern coastal strip is about 30 miles (48 kilometers) wide and consists of a flat plain. Marshy in places but generally fertile, the plain is covered with rich soil carried down from the highlands by rivers and rain. For nearly 1,000 miles (1,610 km), the long east coast runs in a straight, almost unbroken line from southwest to northeast. It consists of white-sand beaches fringed by coral reefs and pounded by the huge breakers that march in endless rows across the southern Indian Ocean.

Calm, saltwater lagoons lie behind most of the island's beaches. Some of these lagoons have been linked together by the Pangalanes Canal, an inland waterway more than 400 miles (644 kilometers) long. Canoes, fishing boats, and small cargo steamers use the canal, which runs between the port of Toamasina in east central Madagascar and the southern city of Farafangana.

In the northeast, the large, deep Bay of Antongil curves into Madagascar's coast. South of the bay is the low, sandy island of Sainte-Marie, 25 miles (40 kilometers) long. Farther south, beyond Farafangana, the eastern coast becomes rocky. The far southeast is broken by hundreds of tiny bays.

From the east coast, the central plateau rises in two huge, steep steps that run nearly the entire length of the island. The first is a rocky bluff called the Betsimisaraka Escarpment, named for the Betsimisaraka people, one of the Malagasy ethnic groups. On top of the nearly 1,000-foot (300-meter) escarpment is a second, even taller bluff: the Great Cliff of Angavo, 1,000 to 2,000 feet (300 to 600 m) high. The top of the Great Cliff forms the eastern edge of the central plateau, a region of spectacular scenery. Madagascar's capital, Antananarivo, is located here.

The plateau reaches 2,500 to 4,500 feet (750 to 1,350 meters) above sea level. Three mountain ranges rise from its rugged terrain. The Massif du Tsaratanana, in the north, includes the island's highest point, the Maromokofro peak (9,436 feet, or 2,830 m). In the center of the island lies Ankaratra, a massive cluster of extinct volcanoes whose highest point is the 8,671-foot (2,601-m) Tsiafajavona peak.

The Andringitra range, in the far south near the city of Faradofay, rises to 8,720 feet (2,616 m) at Pic Boby.

The plateau contains many volcanoes, particularly in the region of Mont d'Ambre in the north, but none have shown any activity since settlement of the island began. In some places, highland lakes (including the large lakes Itasy and Aloatra) have formed in the ancient volcanoes' craters. Near Antsirabe, a city in the center of the plateau, steam rises from dozens of hot springs that French colonists once used as health resorts.

Many short, rapid rivers flow eastward from the central plateau's steep slopes. Some become waterfalls or rapids and drain into the sea over the Great Cliff and the Betsimisaraka Escarpment. Others have carved paths through the cliff walls to empty into the coastal lagoons. The most important rivers are the Bemarivo, the Mananara, the Mangoro, and the Maningory.

Farmland is at a premium. The Malagasy make the most of the available land by terracing hillsides for planting.

The island's southern portion is mostly dry. Although its many gullies and ravines fill with water for a few months during the rainy season, there are only a few year-round rivers: the Mandrare, the Menarandra, and the Linta. The region has no lakes. Farther south, the Betsimisaraka Escarpment and the Great Cliff of Angavo merge into a single wall of rock that hangs steeply out over the sea. The cliff ends at Cape Sainte-Marie, the southernmost tip of Madagascar. Beyond the cape lies empty ocean that stretches for 3,000 miles (4,830 kilometers) to Antarctica.

The island's western zone is between 60 and 125 miles (97 and 201 kilometers) wide. It consists of many ranges of low hills with wide plains between them. The region's rivers—the Sofia, the Onilahy, the Mangoky, the Tsiribihina, the Betsiboka, and others—are longer, wider, and slower than those of the east. They flow across the plains carrying a huge amount of soil eroded from the volcanic highlands. Most of the west coast's rivers have many mouths, all partially blocked by sandbanks that have built up as the rivers deposited their loads of sediment. Each time a sandbank closes off one mouth, the river cuts through the swamps and beaches to form another.

The western region's largest lakes are Ihotry and Kinkony. Unlike the steep cliffs of the eastern seacoast, the western plains slope gradually down to the Mozambique Channel. Sand dunes and mangrove swamps line the western coast; many small bays and coves fill the northwest. Offshore, coral reefs rise in places and small coastal islands—the tips of extinct volcanoes—jut through the water. The largest of these islands is Nosy Be, 8 miles (13 kilometers) off the coast in the Bay of Ampasindava in the northwest. Its wooded peak, called Kokobe, rises 1,075 feet (323 meters) out of the sea.

The islands of Sainte-Marie off the east coast and Nosy Be off the west are large enough to support inhabitants, but Madagascar's coastal waters also contain a handful of tiny, uninhabited islands in

The island of Nosy Be lies off the northwestern coast.

the Mozambique Channel: Nosy Mitsio, the Radama Islands, Chesterfield Island, and the Barren Islands. Fishermen sometimes land on these rocks during storms, and biologists visit them to study birds and fish.

Climate and Weather

Madagascar lies south of the equator, so its seasons are the opposite of the seasons in the United States and Europe. Summer lasts from November until April and is hot and wet. The dry season, from May to October, is Madagascar's winter, although it never gets very cold. Snow is unknown, even on the mountain peaks. July is the coolest month, with temperatures between 50° and 78° Fahrenheit (10° and 25° Centigrade). In December, the hottest month, temperatures range from 61° to 84° F (16° and 29° C).

Throughout the year, temperatures are highest in the northwest and along the east coast. At Antsiranana, a city at the northern tip of the island, temperatures average 81° F (27° C). The southern part of the island is almost as hot, with an average temperature of 73° F (23° C) at Faradofay. In the interior, temperatures are cooler year-round because of the greater altitude. The average annual temperature at Antananarivo, on the central plateau, is 63° F (17° C).

The island's rivers twist over its rocky landscape, forming spectacular waterfalls.

Madagascar's weather and rainfall are controlled by two wind systems: the trade winds and the monsoon. The trade winds blow in from the southeast. Although they blow all year long, they are strongest from May to October. They carry rain that falls mostly on the east coast. Maroantsetra, on the Bay of Antongil, is the wettest place on the island because of the rain carried by the trade winds; it receives 147 inches (3,734 millimeters) of rain each year. As the trade winds move westward across the plateau, they lose their remaining moisture in the form of mist and drizzle. By the time they reach the western part of the island, they are dry.

The monsoon wind blows out of the northwest during the hot, humid months from November to April. It brings rainstorms to the northwest coast and the plateau, but little rain falls in the south. The northwestern island of Nosy Be receives 83 inches (2,108 millimeters) of rain yearly, whereas the city of Morondava, in the central part of the west coast, receives only 30 inches (762 mm). Toliary, on the arid southwest coast, gets a mere 14 inches (356 mm). The central plateau receives moderate rainfall: 53 inches (1,346 mm) each year at Antananarivo and 48 inches (1,219 mm) at Fianarantsoa, a city 200 miles (322 kilometers) south of the capital.

In addition to the trade winds and the monsoon, Madagascar is also subject to terrible tropical cyclones that occasionally form far out over the Indian Ocean. Occurring mostly between December and March, these cyclones blow onto Madagascar's east coast, bringing torrential rains, high winds, and flood conditions. In the days before meteorologists could monitor storms in their early stages, these unpredictable cyclones often devastated the island. Today, advance warnings prepare islanders for the storms, greatly reducing the chance of damage.

Plant and Animal Life

Two hundred million years ago, the land mass that is now the island of Madagascar separated from the African continent. Traveling at the rate of a fraction of an inch (centimeter) per year, the island began its slow journey eastward. Isolated from the forms of life that evolved elsewhere, Madagascar became the home of many species of plants and animals found nowhere else in the world. Over the ages, some species that are common in other parts of the world developed into strange subspecies in Madagascar.

The island's trees include some unique species and some specialized variations of common species. At one time, much of the island was covered with forest: evergreen trees grew in the highlands, leafy trees on the western plains and the eastern escarpment, and palms and other tropical trees along the coasts. Today, islanders have cut down most of the trees for fuel or building materials or to clear land for farming. The plateau has suffered the worst deforestation (and, because trees are no longer holding the topsoil in place, the worst erosion). Much of the island's valuable timber has been exported, although pockets of thick forest remain, especially on the eastern escarpment. Grasses, bamboo, or small, scrubby trees now cover about 85 percent of the island's surface. Screw pines, palmetto bushes, and reeds of various sorts blanket the coastal lowlands.

The traveler's tree grows throughout the island. Its thick, spongy trunk, divided into compartments with corklike walls, holds a great deal of water. The tree's name comes from the fact that thirsty travelers, desperate for water, can cut into the trunk and obtain a pint or so of liquid to drink. (Although the liquid has an unpleasant taste, it can save a person from dying of thirst.) The tree also produces long, tough leaves that can be used to thatch the roofs of traditional Malagasy houses.

The traveler's tree is a xerophyte, a plant especially adapted to survive drought. Madagascar's dry southern region—a desert area called the "Land of Thirst" by the Malagasy—contains many other xerophytes. Some of them are unique to the island; others, such as the 25-foot- (8-meter-) tall organ-pipe cactus, are related to plants found in other dry areas.

One cactus, the prickly pear, was introduced from Mexico in 1796. It thrived in Madagascar and, by holding the scarce rainwater in the ground, transformed much of the southern wasteland into fertile territory where crops and cattle thrived. Unfortunately, a

Thanks to heavy rainfall, tropical plants flourish along the coasts.

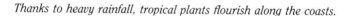

French colonist near Toliary introduced the cochineal insect, also from Mexico, in 1925. The insect, which was used by the Mexicans to create a profitable dye industry (the crushed bodies of the female insects form a rich, red dye), has no natural enemies in Madagascar. As a result, it swept voraciously through the fields of prickly pear cacti and devoured every one. The region's water level fell, ponds dried up, crops withered, and hundreds of people and cattle died of thirst and hunger. Within two years, the region had once again become an inhospitable desert.

The Land of Thirst contains many types of thorn trees unique to Madagascar. The *fantsilotra* is adorned with many rows of steel-hard thorns that grow 3 inches (7.6 centimeters) long, in spiral patterns. Another thorn tree exudes a white, milky sap that burns the skin and causes blindness. The didierea grows in tall, tangled thickets that are almost impossible to penetrate; its thorny branches look like the tentacles of an octopus. People very seldom enter these eerie thorn forests—in fact, some Malagasy believe them to be the home of the dead, forbidden to the living. When French colonists tried in the mid-1600s to establish a settlement called Fort Dauphin at the site of present-day Faradofay, they were sometimes driven into the thorn forests by attacking Malagasy. Many were impaled or poisoned by the strange plants. The few survivors of these raids fled back to France with tales of man-eating trees.

Less sinister is the pachypodium, a smooth-skinned, gourdlike plant about the size of a pumpkin. It stores water in its hollow center and grows entirely above ground, with no roots. Nothing like it is found outside of Madagascar. The most common plant of the south is the baobab, a tree found throughout most of Africa and part of Asia. In Madagascar, however, it grows in a unique form. Elsewhere, the baobab has a narrow trunk and a broad crown of spreading branches. Madagascar's baobab reverses the normal proportions: it is shaped like a great, bloated bottle, with a trunk as much as 75 feet (23 meters) wide but only 60 feet (18 m) tall, topped with a tiny cluster of twiglike branches. Called by the Malagasy "the big-bellied mother of the forest," the baobab is not a good source of fuel or building material because its wood is pulpy and damp. The tree is not entirely useless, however. Its fruit, called "monkey bread," can be brewed into a mildly alcoholic beverage. And some groups among the southern Malagasy carve the trunks of living baobabs into tombs for their dead.

In contrast to the forbidding thorn forests, Madagascar's plant life also includes many beautiful and useful species, especially in the north. Orchids, wildflowers, and flowering bushes and trees are abundant. Some Madagascan species, such as the flowering flamboyant tree, appear today in gardens as far away as Florida and California. Others produce rare oils used in perfumes and prized spices, including vanilla and cloves.

The Great Red Island's animal life is as strange and varied as its vegetation. Madagascar is home to about 40 species of lemurs, tree-dwelling mammals descended directly from the early primates who also evolved into apes and humans. The smallest lemurs are

A few huge trees still remain, although much of the island has been deforested.

about the size of cats; the largest are similar to middle-sized monkeys. Fossils from the island show that lemurs as big as average-sized humans were common until a few thousand years ago, but became extinct before people arrived on Madagascar.

Lemurs have thick fur, bushy tails, and toes designed for gripping. Because some species of lemur are nocturnal (active at night) or crepuscular (active at dusk and dawn), they have large eyes that enable them to see in the dark. Some eat fruit, whereas others dine on insects and small lizards. They climb and jump from tree to tree with great ease and grace, and they are popular in zoos around the world. The destruction of the forests where they live has caused a serious decline in the lemur population. Today, most of Madagascar's surviving lemurs live in protected reserves and national forests.

Several unique species of tiny, insect-eating creatures also live in Madagascar. Called tenrecs, these shy, spiny mammals resemble porcupines. They are small enough to fit in a person's hand—but they are liable to leave a few sharp, little quills in the skin of those who try it.

Madagascar's first human settlers brought dogs and chickens that now thrive in all parts of the island. But by far the most common animal on the island is the zebu, a type of cattle that traders probably brought across the Mozambique Channel from Africa many hundreds of years ago. The zebu have large humps of fatty tissue behind their heads and long, curving horns. They are much prized by the rural Malagasy, who measure wealth and status by the number of cattle a family owns.

No large carnivores or other dangerous land animals live in Madagascar. The island's only fierce animals are the river-dwelling crocodiles. Over the centuries, the Malagasy have ruthlessly hunted the crocodiles for their meat and skin, and now they survive only in remote streams and swamps—with one exception. Near Anivarano Nord, a small town about 30 miles (48 kilometers) south of Antsiranana, is a lake filled with fat, happy crocodiles that nearby villagers feed and worship. The people say that long ago, a wayfarer passed through the village and asked for a drink. The villagers all refused him water—except for one kind woman. The stranger warned the woman to leave the village, and then magically caused it to be submerged in the lake. All of the other villagers were transformed into crocodiles. The woman's descendants, who now live nearby, believe that the crocodiles are their dead relatives and that they have great powers. Therefore, the villagers frequently use the music of drums and flutes to get the attention of the great reptiles, then place fresh cattle-meat on the ground to lure them onto the shore. When a crocodile comes out of the lake for the meat, the villagers—from a safe distance—plead with it to grant them favors and good luck.

Crocodiles are not the only reptiles on Madagascar. Snakes are common. One species, the *do*, ranges in length from 10 to 13 feet (3 to 4 meters); like all the island's snakes, it is harmless. Madagascar also has many varieties of lizard, including several species of chameleon, whose color changes to blend with tree bark, leaves, or earth.

Madagascar is a butterfly collector's paradise. About 800 species thrive on the island. Many moths, including the rare uraniid moth, also live there. Many of Madagascar's postage stamps portray these colorful insects. Madagascar also has many types of spiders, but none are known to be poisonous.

The island's birds include flamingos, egrets, Asian robins, partridges, herons, pigeons, cuckoos, and hawks. Perhaps the most noteworthy bird, however, has been extinct for many centuries. It is the aepyornis, the largest bird ever known. Fossil bones show that a full-grown aepyornis male stood 10 feet (3 meters) tall and probably weighed more than 1,000 pounds (450 kilograms). The aepyornis resembled a huge ostrich in appearance, with a long neck, a heavy body, and long, powerful legs. It was doubtless a fast runner. Like

Zebu, a type of cattle found throughout Africa, are highly valued by the Malagasy.

the ostrich, the aepyornis was a flightless bird—its tiny wings could never have lifted it off the ground.

No reliable record exists of anyone ever having seen a live aepyornis. But their tough-skinned, leathery eggs, hundreds or thousands of years old, still turn up frequently in southern Madagascar. As early as 1850, the first specimen of such an egg reached France. It was more than 1 foot (.3 meter) long and had a capacity of 2.5 gallons (9.5 liters)—8 times the volume of an ostrich egg. Scientists greatly desired to capture a live aepyornis, but they were unsuccessful. Although rumors occasionally tell of giant birds glimpsed in the island's most desolate regions, scientists now believe that the aepyornis lived from about 1 million years ago to about 1,000 or 1,200 years ago. It became extinct soon after the first humans arrived on the island; these early settlers probably feasted on the eggs and young chicks. All that remains of the aepyornis today are a few bones and hundreds of thousands of shattered eggshells carpeting some of the southern beaches and gullies. Once in a while, a rainstorm washes the sand away to reveal a rare, unbroken egg.

Using canoes hollowed out by hand, the Malagasy fish for grouper, whiting, and other varieties of fish in the island's lakes and rivers.

Madagascar's rivers and streams contain rainbow trout, black bass, and tilapia (an edible fish similar to perch). Giant crawfish up to 10 inches (25 centimeters) long live in some mountain brooks and are considered a delicacy by the Malagasy. The island's lagoons, river mouths, and offshore waters are also rich in grouper, tuna, sardines, whiting, crabs, shrimp, mussels, and oysters. Two species, the spiny globefish and the cofferfish, exist only in Madagascan waters. The Indian Ocean is notorious for the great number of sharks that live in its waters, and sharks, including the dreaded great white shark, are common in the waters around Madagascar.

The Great Red Island's most famous fish is the coelacanth (pronounced SEE-la-canth), the "living fossil." A large, ugly fish about

6 feet (1.8 meters) long and weighing about 150 pounds (68 kilo-grams), the coelacanth is armored in heavy, blue-gray scales and has a huge, gap-toothed mouth. But the most remarkable thing about it is that until 1938 scientists believed the coelacanth had become extinct millions of years ago.

Coelacanths swam in all the world's oceans 300 million years ago. In fact, they were closely related to the very first creatures that left the sea for life on land. When paleontologists (scientists who study fossils) first examined fossil traces of ancient coelacanths, they decided that the fish had flourished for 60 or 70 million years, then had died out more than 200 million years before the start of human life. But the coelacanth was not extinct: it continued to swim about in the cold, dark waters of the Mozambique Channel.

In 1938, South African fishermen hauled up a huge fish in the nets of their trawler. The strange creature did not look as if it would be good to eat, and the fishermen wanted to throw it overboard. But one man decided to keep it, and later sent it to an English librarian. Eventually, to the amazement of scientists the world over, it was identified as a coelacanth. Since then, several dozen coelacanths have been brought up. Fishermen from Madagascar and the nearby Comoros Islands have learned that museum curators eagerly seek these useless fish, so they no longer throw them back into the sea when they catch them. Scientists agree that of all living creatures, the coelacanth has survived longest with the least amount of change. For some reason, it is found nowhere but near Madagascar.

Madagascar's early history was dominated by powerful kingdoms, whose leaders constantly competed for control of the island and the Malagasy people.

Early History and the Colonial Era

Madagascar's first inhabitants, the Malagasy, migrated to the island 1,500 years ago from Malaysia and Indonesia, 3,600 miles (5,796 kilometers) to the east. Anthropologists now know that the ancient Indonesians built large, sturdy canoes that could make extremely long sea voyages. Over the course of many centuries of seafaring, these Indonesian travelers populated many distant islands in the Pacific Ocean. Today, scientists believe that Madagascar's original inhabitants may have been the survivors of a single, epic voyage of exploration and colonization.

Other Indonesian and Malaysian groups later came to the island by way of southeast Africa, where some of them had intermarried with the African Bantu peoples. Still other settlers came from Arabia and the Arab settlements in North Africa. But the majority of the island's people are of Malaysian-Indonesian ancestry. Archaeological evidence, such as ancient campfires, settlements, and burial grounds, shows that much of the island was inhabited by the 10th century A.D. At that time, Arab traders began making occasional visits to Madagascar in their dhows, cargo-carrying sailing vessels. They traded cloth and metal goods to the Malagasy in return for spices and slaves.

In 1500, the first European known to have landed on Madagascar arrived—a Portuguese navigator named Diogo Dias. Other Portuguese ships also landed on the island during the 16th century, usually to raid the Malagasy villages for food and women. The Portuguese (who called Madagascar the Isle of St. Lawrence) hoped to drive the Arabs out of their trading posts on the island's northern shores and establish claim to Madagascar. But they were unsuccessful, and the island remained fair game for the other European powers. One of those powers, France, decided to make Madagascar its own.

In 1643, the French established the colony of Fort Dauphin on Madagascar's southeast coast. It lasted only until 1674, when the colonists abandoned it after repeated attacks from Malagasy tribesmen. Despite the shortness of his stay, one of Fort Dauphin's military

The Portuguese sailed into Madagascar to raid villages and drive out Arab traders.

governors, Etienne de Flacourt, had time to write the first lengthy description of the geography and people of Madagascar. Although it was not very accurate, his book was very popular in Europe and excited much interest in the island.

Despite the public's fascination, the French turned their attention away from Madagascar during the late 17th and early 18th centuries, concentrating instead on the Mascarene and Comoros Islands, its smaller and less hostile neighbors. Thus abandoned, Madagascar became the haunt of pirates. The most powerful was a young Frenchman named Misson, who persuaded the crew of a French frigate to join him in founding a pirate society on the shores of the great bay of northern Madagascar (now the site of Antsiranana). Like a Robin Hood of the open seas, he led his men in raids against the rich merchant ships that plied the Indian Ocean. They took no prisoners and killed only when they had no choice—they even freed any slaves they found aboard the ships they captured.

Misson named his pirate city Libertalia and ran it as a democracy, just about the only one of its time. Its fame soon spread across the seas. He invited other pirates to join him, and he even sent out printed pamphlets to recruit new "citizens." In 1697, the infamous Captain William Kidd visited Libertalia. Although Kidd declined to remain in the pirate paradise, half his crew deserted him and joined Misson.

A few years later, an army of Malagasy warriors—angry because many of their women had left them to live with the pirates—destroyed Libertalia. Misson survived, but what happened to him afterwards is unclear. No one knows when or how he died. His ship, *The Victory*, was last seen in the Mozambique Channel. It most likely tore out its keel on a coral reef and went to the bottom in a storm.

During their first few centuries of contact, the Europeans introduced the Malagasy to firearms, which they traded for slaves and spices. Certain Malagasy chieftains used these new weapons to build

These men are descended from the clanspeople who built warlike kingdoms in the 17th century.

up powerful kingdoms that changed the structure of Malagasy society. Instead of many small, independent clans scattered across the island, Madagascar soon had several warlike states bent on conquering their neighbors. During the 17th century, the Sakalava people of the south spread northward and westward, and the Antemoro tribe of the interior conquered the Tanala and Betsileo tribes. In the 18th century, Ratsimilaho, the son of an English pirate and a Malagasy woman, founded the Betsimisaraka kingdom on the east coast. But the most important development in Malagasy politics was the rise of the Merina tribe, an inbred clan of light-skinned Malagasy.

The Merina kingdom arose in the late 1500s in the Ikopa Valley, a swampy region in the center of the island. The Merina were fierce warriors, and their kingdom grew—by the 18th century, their capital of Antananarivo was the island's largest city. For many years, the kingdom was divided among four chieftains vying for power, but finally, in 1797, the Merina were united under King Andrianampoinimerina (the name, which is unusually long even for the Malagasy language, means "the beloved prince of Imerina"). Andrianampoinimerina created uniform laws for the entire kingdom and obtained guns for his army by selling his enemies to the French, who had established several flourishing trade settlements on the eastern coast. He also divided Merina society into three classes: the Andriana, or noble rulers; the Hova, or free men; and the Andero, or slaves. (The Merina as a whole sometimes called themselves the Hova.)

Andrianampoinimerina hoped to unite the whole island of Madagascar under one rule. His favorite saying was "Ny riaka no valamparihiko"—"The sea shall be the limit of my rice field." But he died in 1810 before he could achieve this ambition. His son and heir, Radama I, was a weak ruler who was afraid his own nobles might overthrow him. To preserve his position, he formed an alliance with the British through Sir Robert Farquhar, the British governor of the nearby island of Mauritius.

With British help, Radama soon conquered the entire island, except for a few small regions in the south and west. The French were driven out, keeping hold only of the tiny island of Sainte-Marie. (Radama was too clever to break off relations with them completely—he felt he might someday need their support against the

King Radama allied himself with the British to drive the French out of Madagascar.

British.) Radama began to call himself "king of Madagascar." He invited teachers and missionaries to spread Christianity among the Malagasy, and Madagascar started to become Europeanized.

In 1828, Radama died suddenly. It was said at the time that he cut his throat in a fit of madness brought on by drinking rum. But many believe that he was murdered by his wife, Ranavalona, who was his successor to the throne.

Ranavalona's reign certainly proved her capable of any sort of cruelty or violence. Her first acts were aimed at reversing Radama's Europeanization policy. She deported or slew the missionaries and killed all Malagasy Christians who refused to reject their new faith. She also ended trade and diplomatic relationships with Great Britain and France—although she allowed Jean Laborde, a French citizen, to remain in Madagascar because his engineering skills were useful (he later designed and built a palace for her in Antananarivo).

In 1845, the British and French sent a joint expedition against Ranavalona. Troops landed at Toamasina, but Malagasy soldiers fearlessly fought them off. Perhaps the Malagasy were more afraid of Ranavalona's anger than of the Europeans' bullets.

Ranavalona the Terrible, as she came to be called, executed more than 100,000 of her subjects during her 33-year reign and brought about the deaths of perhaps 1,000,000 more. Some died in battle, but many were victims of her programs of forced labor, in which every adult Malagasy had to work for a year or longer on such projects as roads, bridges, and palaces. Ranavalona's demands were so great, and working conditions so cruel, that the workers died by the thousands. But her most dreadful innovation was the trial-by-ordeal. The queen and her priests devised terrifying methods of torturing anyone suspected of treason, Christianity, or other crimes. Some suspects were forced to swim across crocodile-infested rivers; the priests claimed that if the suspect reached the other side alive he was innocent. Few survived to rejoice in their innocence.

Thousands of servants and soldiers accompanied Ranavalona whenever she appeared in public.

The most common form of trial-by-ordeal was poisoning by *tanghena*, or *tanguin*. The victim was made to swallow this poison, which is made from the oleander plant, and wrapped in bits of chicken skin. The priests then prayed for truth to be revealed. After the prayers, the victim was given a medicinal drink that caused him to vomit up the poison. If he lived, he was innocent. The priests controlled the outcome of the trial by varying the length of their prayers. But even the survivors were crippled by the tanghena trials—blinded, sterilized, or driven mad by the poison. Ranavalona put many thousands of men and women to the tanghena test.

Madagascar was almost entirely cut off from contact with Europe by the time Ranavalona died in 1861. But her son, Radama II, permitted foreigners to return and to set up churches and trade centers. English Protestant and French Roman Catholic missionaries competed to save the souls of the Malagasy. At the same time, foreign merchants gained control over the king through gifts and flattery.

The Merina nobles resented the return of these powerful foreigners and rose against Radama II in 1863. General Rainilaiarivony, the leader of the army, took control of the government and named himself prime minister. He stayed in power for many years by marrying Madagascar's next three rulers in succession: Queens Rasoherina, Ranavalona II, and Ranavalona III. Hoping to modernize Madagascar and make it the equal of the European nations, Rainilaiarivony tried to make Protestantism the state religion and announced new systems of government and education modeled on European practices.

The French, meanwhile, feared that Madagascar was becoming too independent and that they might lose all influence over the Malagasy. They began to trade weapons to the Sakalava people of the south and west, the only Malagasy who had not come under the rule of the Merina kingdom. With this French assistance, the Sakalava fought the Merina in a war that lasted from 1883 to 1885. Afterward,

Radama II allowed foreign missionaries to return and set up Christian churches.

conflict continued to divide those Malagasy who welcomed the French and those who wanted them expelled from the island.

The French claimed that sovereignty over the island was necessary to protect their interests, and Great Britain agreed in 1890. Rainilaiarivony, however, did not share this point of view and refused to submit to the French protectorate. In January 1895, French troops landed on the island. The following September, after only one serious battle, the French captured Antananarivo and exiled Rainilaiarivony to Algeria. They also exiled the last Merina ruler, Queen Ranavalona III. She lived out her days in a small Algerian villa. Her greatest delights in exile were fashionable ballgowns from Paris and expensive perfumes containing the scent of heliotrope from her native island.

Although they had easily defeated the island's rulers, the French faced problems in Madagascar. Some of the highland Merina resisted the French takeover. They formed bands called Menalamba ("red togas") and attempted to stage an armed revolution, but it was stamped out by General Joseph Gallieni, the first French governor-general. In August 1896, France formally voted to annex Madagascar as a colony. The island's colonial history had begun.

Gallieni undertook a systematic program to modernize Madagascar. He abolished slavery and built roads and railroads. French administrators replaced tribal chieftains as local rulers. Gallieni made education compulsory for all male children (although attendance was not often enforced) and ordered that French be taught in all schools. Several tribes outside the Merina region tried to resist the French, but their insurrections were quickly put down. By the time Gallieni left the island in 1905, Madagascar was peaceful—and very French.

During the next 40 years, the French made many efforts to turn Madagascar into an economic asset rather than a liability. They introduced new crops, such as coffee and tobacco. They expanded seaports to handle oceangoing freighters. The Michelin Company of France

Although the French introduced modern construction and agricultural methods to the island, many Malagasy were unhappy with their rule.

even launched an ambitious program to harvest latex from Madagascan rubber trees to use in making automobile tires. (The rubber of Southeast Asia and Indonesia proved to be superior and more economical, however, so the island's rubber industry never got off the ground.) Between 1900 and 1940, the island's population grew from about 2.5 million to 4 million.

Although the French had helped Madagascar's economy grow, not all Malagasy were happy under French rule. Some Malagasy believed that the island should govern itself and formed a secret society called the Vy Vato Sakelika (VVS). It combined ancient tribal religious and magical beliefs with political thinking. Although the French outlawed the VVS in 1915, some branches of it survived.

In 1920 a Malagasy teacher named Jean Ralaimongo—who was probably a VVS member—started a newspaper campaign to persuade France to grant citizenship to the Malagasy. When the French ignored this suggestion, more and more Malagasy began to think about winning their independence. Almost 20 years would elapse before these nationalists found opportunities for action. But the events of World War II would set the stage for independence on the Great Red Island.

During World War II, British and South African soldiers occupied Madagascar.
Soon after the war, the islanders demanded an end to foreign domination.

Independence

In 1940, less than a year after World War II began, France fell to the invading German army. French-ruled Madagascar, therefore, came under the control of the Vichy government, the pro-Nazi regime set up in France. As a result, the Allies (the alliance of Western nations led by Great Britain and the United States) blockaded the island, so that food and other supplies became scarce. In 1942, British and South African troops occupied Madagascar, and eventually the island fell into the control of French administrators who opposed the Vichy government. Before the war was over, Madagascar had rallied behind General Charles de Gaulle's Free French movement.

The war brought Madagascar to the attention of the outside world for the first time in many years. Madagascar's support of the Free French earned General de Gaulle's gratitude, as well as a promise of better treatment from France in the future. In 1945, Madagascar was permitted to elect two representatives to the French Parliament. One year later, France made the island an overseas territory. The Malagasy sent representatives to Paris and elected an assembly to govern the island.

Despite these changes, some of the Malagasy were still not content to remain tied to France—they wanted independence. These nationalists formed the Democratic Movement for the Malagasy Restoration (MDRM). In March 1947, outbreaks of violence in eastern Madagascar signaled the beginning of what the MDRM hoped would be an island-wide rebellion against the French. But the army remained loyal to France; the revolt failed, and more than 11,000 people on both sides were killed.

Although the revolt was unsuccessful, France recognized the need for a change in Madagascar. In 1956, a new act of French law gave its overseas territories the right to elect executives to head their local assemblies. Madagascar elected Philibert Tsiranana, a Malagasy, as its vice premier. After taking office, Tsiranana formed the Social Democratic party (PSD). By managing to get Merina and non-Merina nationalists to work together, he quickly built the PSD into a powerful force.

Two years later, France agreed to let its overseas territories determine their own status. On September 28, 1958, the Malagasy voted overwhelmingly for "autonomy within the French Community" (meaning that they would govern themselves but would continue to uphold trade agreements, currency exchanges, and diplomatic treaties with France and other French territories). Just a few weeks later, on October 14, the Malagasy Republic was declared.

The new republic elected Tsiranana as its president. Although France remained its chief trading partner and many Frenchmen continued to live on the island, the republic cut its remaining ties with France in 1960, becoming completely independent.

During the next 12 years, Tsiranana and his government launched a series of development programs. Inspired by Socialist doctrine, they attempted to redistribute the nation's wealth to make the lives of the rural and peasant Malagasy more bearable. Yet, despite these efforts, some Malagasy felt that independence had not improved their lives. A growing number of Communist sympathizers began to criticize the government. Labor unions, in particular, grew

<51>

powerful and staged strikes and protests against low wages. Student groups objected to the wealthy foreigners who owned property and businesses on the island. In poor health and unable to cope with the growing unrest, Tsiranana resigned from the presidency in 1972. He turned power over to Major General Gabriel Ramanantsoa, who took the title of prime minister.

For the next three years, the republic endured extreme political turbulence. In response to strikes and demonstrations, the Ramanantsoa government tried to reorganize farm ownership along the lines of Russian-style collective farming and then began the policy of nationalizing factories and businesses that continued into the next decade.

The republic's relations with Western nations rapidly deteriorated. Ramanantsoa ordered France to remove all military forces from the island, reclassified French citizens as aliens, and expelled the U.S. ambassador. Meanwhile, he negotiated new treaties and trade agreements with the Soviet Union, China, and other Communist nations.

The atmosphere in the country was thick with rumors of plots, conspiracies, and uprisings. In one tragic episode, Malagasy in the coastal city of Mahajanga, convinced that settlers from the Comoros Islands were plotting to overthrow the government, slaughtered more than 1,400 of them.

These upheavals took their toll, and by 1975, Ramanantsoa had become too unpopular to govern. In February, he resigned, and another

Ramanantsoa nationalized most businesses and expelled the United States ambassador.

army officer, Colonel Richard Ratsimandrava, took over. Six days later Ratsimandrava was assassinated. More riots followed, and the country fell under martial law. The country's military leaders chose Lieutenant Commander Didier Ratsiraka as president and head of a newly formed Supreme Revolutionary Council (SRC). In December, Ratsiraka, newly elected to a seven-year term as president, dissolved the Malagasy Republic and set up the Democratic Republic of Madagascar under a new constitution.

Expanding the Socialist policies of his predecessors, Ratsiraka nationalized the country's banks and mineral resources, and he stressed ties with Communist and radical regimes abroad. In time, however, he was forced to accept Western-style economic reforms demanded by the International Monetary Fund (IMF) as a condition of financial assistance.

Ratsiraka was re-elected to the presidency in 1982 and 1989, but with smaller majorities each time. By the early 1990s, his combination of free-market reforms and authoritarian rule had stiffened opposition among both his political enemies and his traditional supporters. On August 10, 1991, more than 4,000 demonstrators gathered peacefully at the president's palace in suburban Antananarivo to demand that Ratsiraka step down. The Presidential Guard opened fire on the crowd, killing more than 30 and wounding hundreds. Ratsiraka's position became untenable. He agreed to negotiations on the formation of a transitional government. In August 1992, a new constitution was approved by referendum. In February 1993, in a free and fair election, Albert Zafy, leader of the opposition group known as the Forces Vives, was chosen as president.

Zafy and the National Assembly worked to restore political liberties and strengthen civilian control over the military. But Madagascar's economic problems remained as unmanageable as ever, and they would lead to the downfall of the new president.

The government needed foreign aid to meet the payments on a $4 billion debt, but Zafy feared the social cost of further reductions in government jobs and services under the IMF's austerity plan. In desperation he turned to questionable—some would say shady—sources of finance. One

Driven from power in 1993, Didier Ratsiraka returned in 1997 as Madagascar's duly elected president.

scheme involved a $450 million loan from a farmer in Texas, money that the World Bank warned was being laundered by international drug cartels.

As a result of such deals, dissension grew between President Zafy and the leadership of the National Assembly. In 1995, Zafy fired the prime minister. The Assembly responded by impeaching him and removing him from office. The Constitutional High Court upheld the conviction, and a new round of presidential elections began. The winner, announced in February 1997, was former president Didier Ratsiraka, who took office pledging to protect the country's fledgling democracy.

No less than 17 different ethnic groups make up the Malagasy people. Although each group has its own customs and beliefs, all speak the Malagasy language.

Peoples and Ways of Life

The Malagasy are divided into at least 17 distinct ethnic groups. These groups originated as loosely organized clans, each of which occupied a certain region of the island. Each clan kept to itself, and members of the clan married only other clan members. Although the groups are still distinct, travel and marriage among them have increased during the past 100 years, and some of their divisions are becoming blurred. All of the groups regard themselves as equally Malagasy. According to an island saying, "All who live under the sun are plaited together like one big mat."

Madagascar's largest group is the Merina. Their name means "Elevated People," because they were the earliest dwellers in the mountainous region. The next largest groups are the Betsimisaraka ("Inseparable Multitude") and Betsileo ("Invincible Multitude"). Other groups are the Tsimihety ("People Who Do Not Cut Their Hair"), the Sakalava ("People of the Long Valley"), the Antemoro ("People of the Banks"), the Tanala ("People of the Forest"), and the Bara (the meaning of their name is uncertain). The Antandroy ("People of the Thorn Bush") are famed herdsmen whose zebu are the largest and best on the island; the Vezo (another name whose meaning is unknown) live on the west coast and are the island's only great fishermen. The Antanosy ("People of the Island"), the Antaifasy ("People of the Sand"), the Sihanaka ("People of the Lake"), the Antakarana ("People of the Rocks"), and the Benzanozano ("People with Many Braided Hair") are smaller groups. The Betanimena ("People of the Red Soil") are a subdivision of the Merina, and the Mahafaly ("The Joyful People") of the south are Madagascar's finest craftsmen.

One of the problems facing Madagascar's leaders is the long-standing distrust between the Merina highlanders and the coast-dwellers, known as *côtiers*. Most Merina are better educated and wealthier than their countrymen. They had considerably greater power in the colonial government, and today they control Madagascar's economy, outnumbering other groups in businesses and the professions. Since independence, the less privileged lowlanders have tried to keep the Merina out of power, particularly in the civil service, which the *côtiers* now dominate. Former president Albert Zafy was a *côtier* of the Tsimihety group, and the popularly elected National Assembly has given the *côtiers* more proportional representation in government. Although government officials have urged an end to feuds, cooperation between the two groups remains rare.

Land of Tradition

All of Madagascar's groups speak Malagasy, a language related to the native languages of Indonesia and Australia. Although tribes in the south speak a dialect different from that of the central plateau's tribes, they have no trouble understanding one another. But because Malagasy has many long words made up of other words strung together in complicated patterns, outsiders have difficulty learning it.

Malagasy is written in the same alphabet as English and other European languages. The republic has made Malagasy its official language, and in recent years Malagasy books and newspapers have been published. The government realizes that it cannot communi-

(continued on page 65)

SCENES OF
MADAGASCAR

▼ *On some parts of the island, dense forests thrive.*

∧ *Ceramic trinkets, glazed a shiny black, are sold at village markets.*

∧ *Reptiles on Madagascar include varieties of turtles that feed on tropical vegetation.*

▾ Traditional homes were made of mud and thatch; many modern houses are made of wood and tin.

◄ *Flowering bushes color the northern end of the island.*

▼ *The island's warm climate makes it ideal for lizards.*

⋏ *Madagascar is a natural fortress—its steep, rocky shoreline protects the interior.*

⋏ *In Antananarivo, shopkeepers must compete with those who sell their wares on the street.*

➤ *Madagascar is home to more than 40 varieties of lemurs.*

∨ *A baby watches shoppers at his parents' vegetable stand.*

∧ *This woman is one of the Malagasy who have both Indonesian and African ancestors.*

◄ *Traveling musicians entertain in remote villages.*

⅄ *Traditional Malagasy huts are rectangular with thatched roofs; round huts reflect an African influence.*

⋏ *Fishermen row their dugout canoes into the blue Mozambique Channel, a fertile fishing ground.*

➤ *Many of Madagascar's young people must deal with poverty.*

(continued from page 56)

cate with the outside world in Malagasy, however, so all of the country's schools teach French. The government also transacts some of its business in that language.

Madagascar's people share not only a language but also certain traditional aspects of life, such as dress. The chief garment of the early Malagasy was the *lamba*, a shawl or long scarf woven of silk or raffia (a grasslike fiber). Malagasy men wore it over a loincloth; the women wore it over a sarong (a large piece of cloth wrapped around their bodies). Today, the lamba is a proud symbol of independence for the Malagasy. Most wear a lamba across their shoulders even with Western-style dress. Island men typically wear a pair of trousers or knee-length shorts topped with a sleeveless tunic. Women wear dresses or skirts only, never pants. Most clothing is made of imported cotton cloth, often in bright colors and lively prints, but Western-style business suits in dark colors are increasingly common among government workers in Antananarivo and other cities.

Malagasy architecture also reflects old traditions. Unlike African huts and houses, which are almost always round, Malagasy dwellings are always tall and rectangular, with steep, thatched roofs. Rural houses are usually made of mud bricks or woven mats; in some parts of the eastern forest, they are built with bamboo canes and palm fronds. They are generally more spacious and sturdier than the houses of most tropical regions.

In the cities and towns, the well-to-do Malagasy incorporate traditional building designs into their two- or three-story wooden houses, with the kitchen at the top, living quarters in the middle, and storage below. Some larger houses have broad balconies supported by brick columns.

Another tradition shared by all the Malagasy is the caste system that was introduced by the Merina king Andrianampoinimerina. His concept of three divisions of society eventually spread throughout

At the turn of the century, most Malagasy women still wore traditional sarongs.

the island. At one time, every Malagasy considered himself either a noble, a free man, or a slave. Today, most Malagasy ignore these hereditary distinctions, although some highland people still observe them on ceremonial occasions. On these occasions, the islanders revive traditional titles and rules of behavior dating from the 18th century.

Nearly 99 percent of Madagascar's population is Malagasy. The remainder consists of small groups of Comorans, Indians, and Pakistanis and a handful of French and Chinese. The French are generally the proprietors of small, family businesses, such as hotels and restaurants. The Indians, Pakistanis, and Chinese operate little shops or sell goods at booths in the marketplaces.

Madagascar's population is one of the fastest-growing in the world, with 43 births per 1,000 citizens each year (the world average is 24 per 1,000). Although the country is quite poor, the government has discouraged the use of birth control and urged each family to have as many as 12 children. Many Madagascan leaders feel that their island is underpopulated and can support more citizens. They also believe that more workers are needed to develop the country's resources and make it prosperous. But the high birth rate is causing a strain on the island's health-care and educational programs. Nearly half the population is under 15 years of age, and demographers (people who study population trends) predict that soon Madagascar will be virtually an island of teenagers. Life expectancy is short—51 years for men, 53 for women—and only 15 percent of the population is age 45 or over.

Despite its rapid growth, Madagascar is less densely populated than many other underdeveloped countries. It has an average population density of only 62 people per square mile (24 per square kilometer). But much of its terrain is too rugged, dry, or swampy to be farmed or even inhabited, so the population density in good

In the eastern forest, many Malagasy make tall huts out of bamboo.

farming areas is considerably higher. The eastern part of the central plateau and the eastern coastal lowlands are the most heavily inhabited parts of the island. The western two-thirds of the island, however, is lightly populated, and the government hopes to establish new villages and farming centers in this region.

Slightly more than 78 percent of all Malagasy live in the countryside, usually in small villages. Less than 22 percent live in cities and towns. Most young Malagasy seem content to remain in their home villages rather than to flock to the towns in search of jobs and Western lifestyles. Consequently, Madagascar's cities are growing much more slowly than those of other African and Asian countries. When people do migrate within the country, they usually move from one rural location to another.

Long ago, highland tribes such as the Merina and the Betsileo perched their villages on hilltops and dug moats or ditches around them for defense. Today, Madagascar's villages are scattered across valley floors as well. In these small, country towns, most people keep at least a few zebu and many cultivate farm plots. Farmers grow rice on valley floors and on hillsides that can be irrigated; layers of terraced rice fields cover many slopes. In years past, the Malagasy practiced slash-and-burn agriculture: they would cut and burn the trees away from a section of forest, build a village, farm the area for a few years until the soil lost its fertility, and then move to a new spot a few miles away. The government is trying to discourage slash-and-burn farming because it has destroyed much of the island's timber and usually results in severe erosion, but the people have been slow to accept the idea of permanent fields.

City Life

Madagascar's cities and towns are very new, compared to the great cities of Europe, Asia, and the Middle East. Until quite recently, most of them were nothing more than large villages, and even today urban development remains confined to the capital. Antananarivo, the capital and largest city, has 1,000,000 inhabitants, whereas Toamasina, the second largest city, has a mere 200,000. Still, the cities of the Great Red Island have some points of interest.

Antananarivo, called Tana by the Malagasy, surprises visitors who expect a typical, teeming Third World metropolis. Perched on two sheer mountain ridges and built almost entirely in the unique Malagasy style, it is an extremely beautiful city. Its steep, winding, cobblestoned streets run along the edges of terraces carved into the hillsides. Its multilevel houses, with tall roofs overhanging their balconies, appear to be stacked haphazardly almost on top of one another. Except for the blinding white paint used on every building, Tana somewhat resembles a medieval European city.

Antananarivo is the site of a large, modern hospital built in the European style.

Each village has a market, where everything from food to magic charms is sold.

The Manjakamiadana Palace of Queen Ranavalona the Terrible dominates the city's skyline. French engineer Jean Laborde built the palace, whose name means "Where It Is Comfortable to Reign," in 1839. On orders from the queen, Laborde constructed a traditional Malagasy wood-and-thatch cabin on a grand scale.

Laborde realized that to create a traditional home, he needed to begin with a master post, which the Malagasy use to hold up the roof beams. To find a suitable master post, Laborde sent crews of slaves into the forests of the Betsimisaraka Escarpment. There they found a massive ebony tree, which they felled and then transported up to the plateau. Many slaves died during the agonizing trip. The post they wrought from the tree measures 129 feet (39 meters) in height and is so thick that two men cannot join hands around it. The Malagasy still call this post Vola Mihitsy ("Worth Its Weight in Gold").

Little of Laborde's strange structure is visible today. A few years after the palace was completed, Ranavalona decided that she should have a stone palace, like those of the European kings and queens of whom she had been told. She ordered James Cameron, a Scottish missionary and architect, to build an outer layer of stone around her palace. He provided the Manjakamiadana with a tile roof, turrets, dormer windows, Roman arches, and a mishmash of other architectural styles. There is no building quite like it anywhere in the world. Madagascar preserves it as a national monument.

The heart of Tana, as of all Malagasy cities, towns, and villages, is the central marketplace. At one time, Friday was market day in Tana. As the Malagasy word for Friday is "Zoma," the market eventually came to be known by that name, although now it is busy every day. Zoma is a crowded jumble of open-air stands where merchants offer everything from bridal veils to zebu-horn spoons, from dried fish to magic amulets. Customers include housewives buying family meals, government workers negotiating to buy their lunches, and students browsing the stalls with books under their arms. It is usually a peaceful, colorful scene, although during periods of civil disturbance, Tana's riots always seem to start in Zoma.

An important city in the north is Antsiranana, which has a population of about 80,000. Many of its inhabitants work at Madagascar's military base, which is located there.

Two historically significant towns are Antsirabe and Faradofay. Antsirabe, in the old Merina region, was a popular resort in the colonial period. Many old French hotels and restaurants remain, and although their elegance is somewhat faded, Malagasy who can afford to travel like to visit this city. Faradofay, in the south, also preserves a relic of earlier French ventures on the island: the 300-year-old ruins of Fort Dauphin.

Meat is a luxury in Madagascar, and a trip to the butcher shop can be very expensive. Rice and vegetables make up the majority of the Malagasy diet.

Customs, Culture, and the Arts

Most Malagasy customs originated in Indonesia, as did the Malagasy themselves. Their food, family life, and religious beliefs greatly resemble those of Pacific Islanders. The Malagasy even cultivate their rice in terraced fields like those found in Indonesia.

Malagasy families tend to live close together, usually with several generations in one house. Women marry in their teens and are responsible for raising the children, tending the gardens or family fields, and doing the shopping, cleaning, and cooking. Men have traditionally been cattle herders, but today many work on large, state-owned rice farms. Others hold office or factory jobs.

Malagasy food is very similar to Indonesian food. Rice—usually fried or steamed with chopped vegetables, bits of chicken or beef, and peppers and other spices—is the basis of every meal. Like the food of Southeast Asia, Malagasy dishes are often extremely hot and spicy because they are seasoned with chilies, peppercorns, cloves, garlic, and coriander. Although cattle are numerous, many of them are exported or reserved for religious sacrifices, so meat is rare. When meat is used, it is often shredded into tiny pieces and mixed with rice. Fruit is plentiful, especially along the east coast, where the Malagasy enjoy oranges, lemons, papayas, and bananas.

Because Madagascar was a French colony for a half-century, many Malagasy learned to cook in the European style. Some restaurants in Antananarivo and other cities offer classic French dishes, such as beef tournedos, onion soup, and crepes suzette. But many popular Western foods, such as hamburgers, sandwiches, and salads, are completely unknown.

Although Malagasy culture has little in common with African ways of life, it does include a few elements borrowed from the Islamic Arabs. For example, the names of the days of the week are borrowed from the Arabic language. Another borrowing is an intricate system of fortune-telling called *sikidy*, which gives meaning to numbers and dreams. *Ombiasy* (village wise men) are the most skillful practitioners of sikidy, but all Malagasy understand something of sikidy and refer to it in their daily lives.

Religion and the Cult of the Dead

The Malagasy's ancient religious beliefs still thrive in modern-day Madagascar. Even those who have accepted the Christian and Muslim faiths have not rejected their native beliefs. Rather, they have combined the old religion with the new.

Muslims comprise 5 percent of Madagascar's population, and most live in the coastal cities and towns of the north. About 40 percent of the Malagasy have adopted Christianity. This group is evenly divided between Protestants and Roman Catholics. Most of the island's Protestants are Merina highlanders. Its Catholics are primarily coastal people, especially in the south, where Jesuit monks arrived with the first French settlers. This religious difference contributes to the conflict between the highlanders and the côtiers.

Over half of the population has retained the ancestral Malagasy religion. The religion does not have a name or a formal doctrine. It consists of habits and beliefs handed down over the past several thousand years by the ombiasy, who act as priests or magicians.

Traditional Malagasy religious practices include the use of idols like this one.

The core of the Malagasy religion is reverence for ancestors. The Malagasy believe in one god, called Zanahary ("the Creator") or Andriamanitra ("The Perfumed Lord"). They believe that their dead ancestors (or *razana*) can obtain favors from Zanahary for the living—or punishment in the form of illness or bad luck if the living do not show respect for the dead. All ancestors, including very distant ones, must be remembered and praised. For example, almost all Malagasy worship King Andrianampoinimerina, who died in 1810, as an ancestor. Even many Christian Malagasy believe that the spirits of their ancestors are near them at all times, watching, protecting, and advising them. They believe that the spirits of the dead remain active in their communities.

The Malagasy show respect for ancestors in two important ways. One is sacrifice. A family will kill chickens or, more often, zebu on the anniversary of an ancestor's death, on various holy days, and whenever the ombiasy indicates that the spirits need a gift. Family members offer the meat to the spirits; later, the family usually eats it.

The other way the Malagasy worship their ancestors is by building elaborate tombs, called cold houses. These large, stone tombs look like rooms that are half-buried in the ground. The tombs of especially powerful people are often decorated with zebu horns ob-

People who practice the Malagasy religion participate in many religious ceremonies.

tained during sacrifices. Thousands of horns surround some old tombs.

The Malagasy believe it is extremely important to be buried near their relatives. The greatest insult a Malagasy can receive is the wish that his skull "may never lie alongside the skulls of the ancestors." When a Malagasy dies far from home, his family will do everything in its power to bring the body home for burial in the family cemetery.

Perhaps the most important ritual of the Malagasy religion is the *famadihana*, or "turning over the dead." Every four or five years, families open their ancestors' tombs, take out the bodies, wrap them in new lambas of fine silk, and carry them through the streets in a parade. Family members and villagers dance and sing because they regard the famadihana as a joyful reunion with the dead one. They sacrifice some zebu and hold a feast, then they rebury the ancestors

with prayers. Every ancestor, however long dead, receives this mark of honor periodically. Christian Malagasy usually take the body to church for a blessing as part of their famadihanas. Often, their ministers or priests will accept the invitation to take part in the ritual.

Other traditional religious beliefs and superstitions influence the daily lives of all Malagasy. For example, no Malagasy would dream of building a house or going on a journey without asking the local ombiasy or *mpanandra* (astrologer) for the luckiest day on which to start. Nor would a Malagasy disobey a *fady*, or taboo (a prohibition against some activity that is believed to anger the spirits). Sometimes a fady conflicts with other social pressures. For example, the village ombiasy may declare a fady against working in the rice fields on a particular day, even though the government calls for increased rice production. He may also caution against going to school, although the law requires that all children attend. Or he may announce that an old footpath is now taboo and a new path must be made to replace it, even though the new path will make the trip between two points longer. No matter what the fady, many Malagasy, especially in the more remote country villages, find it almost impossible to act against it.

Despite the Malagasy's occasional difficulties in combining ancient beliefs with modern life, religion remains a strong, healthy feature of their society. Out of respect for the razana, families remain close and children honor their parents. The basic similarity of belief among all Malagasy (even those who have been converted to foreign religions) helps to unify the different ethnic groups.

Traditional Crafts

Traditional Malagasy arts have survived in most parts of the island, although they often show some recent Western influences. For example, traditional Indonesian musical instruments such as the zither, the conch horn, and the cone-shaped drum are still widely played, but folk music now includes Christian church hymns adapted to the Malagasy style of chanting.

Another traditional art form that the Malagasy still practice is wood carving. The Betsileo people have developed a thriving business making inlaid furniture from the island's precious woods, including ebony, rosewood, and sandalwood. The Mahafaly people are perhaps the island's most creative carvers. They build tombs of colored stones and decorate them with a unique kind of carving called the *aloalo*

("tomb posts"). These posts, often as tall as 20 feet (6 meters), are tree trunks or thick poles similar to American Indian totem poles. Carvings on the posts have mystical meanings and also tell the story of the dead person's life. For example, one scene might show a child in a schoolroom, learning his ABCs; above it may be a carving of a canoe representing a journey, a pair of doves showing that the person had a happy married life, or a humped and horned zebu symbolizing wealth. The Malagasy sometimes call these posts "soul perches," for they believe that the spirits of the dead sit atop them to survey the world of the living. Although the Malagasy would never disturb a tomb, travelers and art collectors eagerly snatched up many of the posts during the colonial period. Today, it is illegal to remove authentic tomb posts. Instead, tourists can purchase small replicas of them in souvenir shops.

Intricately carved wooden posts, called aloalo *("tomb posts"), mark the graves of the Mahafaly people. Each post tells a story.*

The Betsileo women have become skilled weavers, producing mats and cloths of raffia fiber for export as well as for use at home. They also make colored straw hats that are now popular everywhere on the island. Betsileo and Merina women also practice embroidery, sewing, and dressmaking, skills that they learned from the French.

The government has established ministries of cultural affairs and traditional arts to encourage the Malagasy to retain their arts and customs while experimenting with new ones. Most recently, the government introduced several new national holidays: the Festival of Rice, Independence Day, and the Festival of Trees. Government leaders hope that these seasonal and political festivals will promote unity among the Malagasy.

Other institutions also support culture and the arts in Madagascar. Churches, schools, towns, and private groups hold frequent concerts and dances. Malagasy who move to Antananarivo or other cities can join cultural clubs based on their home districts. Antananarivo has a number of libraries, including the National Archives, the Bibliothèque (French for "library") Municipale, the Bibliothèque Nationale, and the library of the University of Madagascar. The university museum and other museums feature exhibits of Madagascan culture, archaeology, and biology.

Before the Europeans arrived, writing was unknown in Madagascar. Literature consisted of spoken poetry, folktales, and chants in praise of Zanahary or of great warriors of the past. Although islanders treasured the few manuscripts left by Arabic traders, they were unable to read them. In 1820, however, the London Missionary Society introduced the Latin alphabet and the printing press to Madagascar. Since then, the islanders have developed a thriving printing industry. Today, publishers print books and newspapers in Malagasy and French.

By the time the nation gained its independence, a Malagasy literature had developed. Today, although few people outside of the country know of the Malagasy authors, many of their countrymen read their works. The most important Malagasy writers have been the poets Jacques Rabemananjara, whom the French exiled to Paris in the 1950s because he was a nationalist, and Flavien Ranaiavo, who served as the island's director of information during the 1960s. Young writers today are experimenting with Western-style novels and plays. Before long, perhaps, a Malagasy author will win a world-wide audience for his or her stories of life on the Great Red Island.

A Malagasy woman votes in the 1996 presidential election. Since the early 1990s, international observers have noted improvements in the country's electoral and human rights practices.

Government and Society

The 1992 constitution instituted a system of checks and balances designed to prevent any one branch of government from holding too much power. The president is elected to a five-year term and may be re-elected only once. He is responsible primarily for foreign policy and national defense and does not initiate or execute domestic legislation.

That responsibility is entrusted to the head of the government, the prime minister, who is appointed by the president, and a council of 29 ministers. The 138-member National Assembly, a group of legislators elected to represent the different regions of the island, makes the country's laws. The ministers and Assembly members serve four-year terms. All men and women aged 18 and over are eligible to vote. The president and ministers, acting together, may dissolve the National Assembly and call for new elections.

A four-level system of elected officials administers local government. The island's thousands of village communities, called *fokolona*, elect representatives to associations of village councils, called *firaisampokontany*. These councils, in turn, elect representatives to district assemblies, called *fivondrynampokontany*. Finally, the district assemblies send delegates to participate in the government of the six administrative provinces into which the island is divided. These provinces, called *faritany*, are Antananarivo, Antsiranana, Fianarantsoa, Mahajanga, Toamasina, and Toliary. Each is centered in the city of the same name.

Madagascar's justice system has improved a great deal since the old days of trial-by-ordeal. There are now civil and criminal courts, courts of appeal, and the Constitutional High Court, the island's equivalent of the Supreme Court of the United States. The modern legal system is modeled on French law codes and practices, adapted where necessary to suit the islanders' needs. When judging cases involving marriage, inheritance, land ownership, and family problems, the magistrates generally take local custom and tradition into consideration.

Madagascar's army consists of about 20,000 troops. As part of their military duties, some army divisions work on public engineering and construction projects. The air force and navy have been combined into the Aeronaval Force, which numbers about 900 men. The naval branch has six vessels, most of which are of French origin. The air branch has 14 fighter planes and 6 helicopters. Much of the armed forces' equipment is out-of-date—some of it is left over from World War II.

The French built this post office; today, the government runs the mail system.

Under Madagascan law, children between the ages of 6 and 11 must go to elementary school.

A separate force of 7,500 men, called the National Gendarmerie, acts as a police force inside the country. Police units are stationed in the provincial capitals and in some of the larger towns. The country villages, where most of the people live, have no permanent police or fire departments. Rather, under the direction of the local leaders, villagers help each other during emergencies. The crime rate is low, so villagers call in the police only when they are needed.

Education

Education is free in Madagascar, and all children between the ages of 6 and 11 are required to attend primary school. In the cities, classes are held in school buildings. In the country, they are often held in churches or religious missions, although the teachers are paid by the state and not by the churches.

Although about 90 percent of the island's children attend school at some point, many do not stay for the full five years. Some leave school because they are needed to work in their parents' fields; others live on remote farms and do not want to leave their families to go to school. Only about 12 percent of the Malagasy go on to secondary school. Nevertheless, Madagascar's literacy rate has risen dramatically in the past 50 years; it now stands at 80 percent. Many more women than men are illiterate, because the Malagasy encourage boys to stay in school and get jobs, but expect girls only to marry and have children. Although the government wants all Malagasy of both sexes to complete their educations, most people still feel that educating girls is less important than schooling boys.

The University of Madagascar is located in Antananarivo and has branches in the capitals of the other five provinces. Enrollment has increased since the mid-1960s. By the mid-1990s, there were 40,000 students at the university. The island also has a college to train teachers, who are in short supply in Madagascar.

Health

Health conditions are poor in Madagascar, despite the island's century-long exposure to Western-style medicine. In 1880, missionaries established a medical school in Antananarivo, but it has since closed. Today, apart from some small, rural clinics and hospitals run by Christian missions, there are few health-care facilities outside the cities. The country also has a severe shortage of doctors—there is only 1 doctor for every 17,000 inhabitants.

Madagascar's biggest health problems are malaria and parasitic infections, such as schistosomiasis. These parasitic diseases are hard to combat, because they breed in the streams from which the Malagasy drink and in the irrigated rice fields in which they work. Leprosy and tuberculosis, common in many tropical climates, also cause many deaths among the Malagasy. Another health threat is posed by venereal diseases, which the first

Established in 1880, the medical college at Antananarivo is now closed.

Europeans brought to the island. The Malagasy seem to be particularly vulnerable to these diseases, and many children are born already infected with them. The government has said that improved health care, along with more thorough educational programs, is one of the most important benefits it hopes to bring to its citizens.

Because Madagascar has few valuable resources and has not developed an industrial economy, most people earn a living by farming and raising livestock.

Economy and Transportation

Explorers who came to the Great Red Island hoping to find it rich in gold, silver, and diamonds were disappointed. Madagascar has none of these valuable natural resources. French and Malagasy prospectors mined some gold in the late 1800s, but the mines gave out long ago. The island does, however, have unusual quantities of certain semiprecious gems, such as amethysts, beryls, tourmalines, and garnets. In fact, garnets are so common in the south that the beach at the mouth of the Menarandra River is covered with crushed garnets. As a result, the sand glitters deep crimson in the sunlight. Unfortunately, Madagascar's garnets and other gemstones are of little value; they are usually polished and sold as souvenirs by village craftsmen.

The island does have a smattering of other minerals, including iron, nickel, copper, coal, lead, graphite, and bauxite. But none of these occurs in sufficient quantity to support a mining industry. Signs of radioactive minerals—thorium and uranium—have been detected in the south and may prove valuable one day.

Reserves of Madagascar's most valuable natural resource, timber, have been drastically depleted over the years. During the colonial period, the French began a program of reforestation, but anticolonial protesters deliberately burned down many of their forests. Today, the government has formed a company to plant millions of seedlings in parts of the plateau and the eastern escarpment that once were heavily forested. A similar company is building dams and electric plants to harness the hydroelectric energy of the eastern waterfalls. Prospectors have discovered some deposits of tar sand (sand that contains petroleum deposits) and oil, but they are difficult to extract from the earth and may not be worth the trouble. Since the 1980s, a variety of U.S., British, and Canadian oil companies have engaged in exploratory drilling, and in 1995 the government took further steps to license and encourage petroleum exploration.

Agriculture—mainly rice farming and cattle herding—employs 88 percent of the population. Rice is the single biggest crop. The country produces more than 2 million tons (2.2 million metric tons) each year, but even this is not enough. Since the 1970s, Madagascar has had to import supplemental rice to feed its people.

The biggest export crops are coffee and vanilla. Madagascar is the world's largest supplier of vanilla. This spice is made from the pod of the vanilla tree, which thrives in the north, near the city of Antalaha. In past years, vanilla growers made huge fortunes from their plantations, but the value of vanilla has fallen recently because many former importers now favor artificial flavorings. Madagascar also exports livestock (mostly zebu) and meat, but the Malagasy have held the industry back by hoarding their cattle until they die of old age and are worthless. In addition, they sacrifice many cattle each year—in 1980, for example, they ritually slaughtered a zebu at the airport in Antananarivo to bring good luck to Air Madagascar's new 747 jet. Such practices make it unlikely that the Malagasy will ever regard their cattle as an economic resource.

Other export crops are pepper, bananas, sugarcane, and tobacco. Cloves and other spices grow on Sainte-Marie Island, once called the Isle of Cloves. Mariners knew they were approaching Madagascar

The beef industry has suffered because zebu have ritual significance for the Malagasy.

when they caught the sweet scent of cloves on the ocean breezes. Nosy Be is another fragrant island. There, workers crush flowers to produce rare oils called ylang-ylang and vetiver, most of which are sold to the great perfume makers of France. All of these crops are sold in marketplaces around the world, but none is large enough to offset the money Madagascar must pay to other countries for petroleum products, machinery, and cloth.

The Malagasy also grow many fruits and vegetables for use in their own kitchens or for sale in village markets. These include apples, avocados, grapefruit, lemons, oranges, plums, pineapples, guavas, corn, beans, peanuts, coconuts, and cassava (a plant whose edible roots can be ground into tapioca flour). Cotton, raffia, and sisal (a fiber used in rope making) support a small weaving industry. The island's other light industries, most of them housed in small factories near Antananarivo, make soap, fertilizer, paper, cigarettes, bricks, and beverages.

Although the waters around the island swarm with edible fish, Madagascar's fishing industry is underdeveloped. Except for the Vezo people, the Malagasy do not have a tradition of large-scale deep-sea

fishing. Coastal villagers tend to fish in the lagoons and the waters close to shore. Those who live inland seldom see or eat ocean fish, although some raise a few carp or trout in their irrigated rice paddies. The government hopes to encourage such at-home fish farming as a good source of inexpensive protein. At the same time, it plans to develop a modern, commercial fishing industry as soon as funds are available for boats and processing equipment.

This coffee-packing plant is one of the light industries that have recently developed.

Through a government-sponsored program, this young man learns to shape wood on a lathe.

Another industry for which the government has high hopes is tourism. At present, few Europeans and almost no Americans visit Madagascar. The country's tourism bureau wants to lure more foreigners and their money to the island, but services such as hotels and resorts will have to improve if tourism is ever to be an important part of the economy.

The principal unit of Madagascar's currency is the Malagasy *franc*, which is divided into 100 *centimes*. Over the past decade, the currency has been devalued. Inflation is high; prices tend to go up by as much as 25 percent each year. Today, it takes about 4,200 francs to equal U.S. $1, and 1 centime is worth about 0.0002 cents.

The average yearly family income is about U.S. $820. A pair of men's shoes costs about U.S. $5. A rural family's income is generally spent on clothing, material to build or repair the house, and religious feasts or ceremonies. Much of the economy, especially in the countryside, is based on trade and barter. Country people grow most of their own food. Medicine is free, and fuel for heating is unnecessary because of the warm climate. Still, most Malagasy are extremely poor by world standards and consider themselves fortunate if they have two sets of clothes and a blanket to call their own. Toys, appliances, and other luxuries are out of the question for any but the wealthiest Malagasy.

Transportation

The Malagasy have always been great walkers. It is not extraordinary for a man or woman to make more than one trip on foot up and down the length of the island during his or her lifetime. Today, walking remains the primary means of transportation. Automobiles are rare, and most Malagasy have never ridden in one. The road system is best on the plateau and in the eastern region. There are few roads in the west. Paved or not, most roads become muddy, flooded, and almost impassable at the height of the wet season.

Railways run north and south on the plateau, and two rail lines connect the plateau with the eastern region. The railroads transport agricultural produce and other goods around the island. They also transport large numbers of people—more and more Malagasy have turned to train travel because tickets are inexpensive. Like its roads, however, Madagascar's rail service is almost nonexistent in the western portion of the country.

Many government officials, businessmen, and tourists can afford to travel by air from one city to the next. Ivato Airport near

Transportation systems are not well developed, but some modern bridges have been built.

Antananarivo is the island's major international airport. Most cities and towns have smaller airstrips for flights within the country.

Toamasina is the island's main commercial shipping port. It has a direct rail line to Antananarivo, as well as many new quays and warehouses. The port at Antsiranana (called Diego-Suarez in colonial times) served as a naval base for the French and is now a military harbor. Mahajanga, on the west coast, is a large harbor, but it is too shallow for deep-water craft. Many dhows (cargo-carrying trading

vessels) from the Comoros Islands and the African coast put in at Mahajanga. In addition to these ports, many deep bays in western Madagascar have the potential to become excellent commercial ports. Unfortunately, Madagascar's present economy is too weak to develop them.

The nation's greatest challenge is to improve conditions in rural Madagascar, where poverty, illiteracy, and disease continue.

Madagascar's Future

The Great Red Island of Madagascar has always seemed somewhat removed from the rest of the world. It broke away from the African continent more than 200 million years ago and, isolated from outside influence, became a world unto itself—a land of exotic plants found nowhere else in the world, a land where animals thought to have died out millions of years ago still thrive.

In Marco Polo's time, Madagascar symbolized the exotic, half-mythical lands that Europeans believed lay just beyond the edge of the known world. Many people refused to believe that such a land could exist. Later, when explorers verified its existence, the island became even more of a puzzle—an African island inhabited by an Asian people, a land of strange customs and beliefs.

Madagascar remained a land of contrasts in the 17th and 18th centuries, when idealistic pirates set up a democratic community from which they pillaged passing ships. Later, it became a land of tribal kingdoms and despotic monarchs. In the 19th century, Madagascar fell under French rule, and yet another influence became part of the island's culture.

By the time independence arrived in the 20th century, Madagascar was more French than African or Asian. But the Malagasy people were not content to live under systems and beliefs borrowed from others, and they began to break the ties that bound them to Europe and the West, and especially France, their former colonial master.

Despite their determination to forge their own nation, the Malagasy remain the products of many influences. Their culture combines the modern with the traditional. Many Malagasy have accepted Christianity, yet maintain Malagasy religious traditions. They have

A tourist trade would provide Malagasy artists with a larger market for their wares.

adopted a Western system of justice, yet take local customs into account when rendering decisions. They wear Western clothing, yet drape the traditional lamba over their shoulders.

The contrasts seem likely to increase as Madagascar attempts to modernize its lifestyle and bolster its economy. Its strange, haunting beauty and its proud, colorful people make the island ripe for tourism. If the island exploits this potential, and if it successfully settles, irrigates, and farms its wide-open western plains, it may yet be able to support itself and to take its place in the world market. Furthermore, if the government's social programs manage to ease some of the basic burdens of the Malagasy people, they may be able to increase their role in national and international politics.

The country has already begun to enter the international arena. It holds membership in the United Nations and the Organization of African Unity. The country's leaders hope that they can use their Asian heritage and African location to serve as a link between Asia and Africa, to help the countries of the two underdeveloped continents pool their knowledge and resources to benefit each other. Although Africa and Asia have historically remained aloof from one another, the Malagasy people have managed to bridge the gaps that separate the two. If they can help increase communication and cooperation among countries of the two regions, the Malagasy and their island could gain immense political and economic importance.

During the 1980s, political experts feared that Madagascar's relationship with the Soviet Union would lead to increased Communist influence on the island. The situation changed late in the decade, however, with the collapse of Communist rule in Eastern Europe and the break-up of the Soviet Union. These events had a direct impact on Madagascar, giving new life to opposition groups and helping to bring on the crisis that led to the reform of the government. Now that the cold war is over, Madagascar is reaching out to many different countries in hopes of attracting investment and trade deals.

In many ways, Madagascar's culture has remained unchanged since the Malagasy first came to the island. But through the influence of the many foreigners who have passed through the country over the centuries, its status is beginning to change. The many contrasts that once tore the island apart may now be used to advantage. Once a remote, unexplored land, Madagascar today is developing the political and economic strength to take its place in the modern world.

‹ G L O S S A R Y ›

Aepyornis   The largest bird ever known, about 10 feet (3 meters) tall. It lived on Madagascar from 1 million years ago until soon after the first human inhabitants arrived. Today, the only remains of the aepyornis are fossil bones and eggs.

Aloalo   Carved, wooden tomb posts, produced by the Mahafaly people, that tell the story of the dead person's life or incorporate mystical symbols.

Coelacanth   A 6-foot (2-meter) fish found only in the deep waters of the Mozambique Channel. The coelacanth dates from about 300 million years ago and was believed extinct until 1938, when a live specimen was caught by a group of South African fishermen.

Cold houses   Elaborate, above-ground tombs that are part of the practice of ancestor worship.

Côtiers   French for "coast-dwellers." The côtiers are generally poorer and somewhat less educated than the residents of the highlands. Conflict between the two groups plagues Malagasy society and government today.

Dhows   Arab cargo boats used in the Indian Ocean trade from the 8th century A.D. to the present. They have distinctive, triangular sails.

Fady   A taboo or prohibition set forth by the ombiasy. Most Malagasy are extremely reluctant to disobey a fady, even though it may conflict with other laws or social pressures.

Famadihana	The ceremony of "turning over the dead," in which the Malagasy honor their dead relatives with new lambas and ceremonial parades every four or five years.
Faritany	The six administrative provinces of the island.
Firaisampokontany	Associations of village councils that are elected by the members of the fokolona.
Fivondrynampokontany	District assemblies consisting of members elected by the firaisampokontany.
Fokolona	Village communities.
Lamba	A shawl or long scarf made of silk or grassy fibers. It is the traditional garment of the early Malagasy, and many islanders today wear it as a symbol of national pride.
Lemurs	Tree-dwelling mammals descended from the early primate ancestors of apes and humans. About 40 species of lemurs live on Madagascar.
Mpanandra	An astrologer whom many Malagasy consult to find a lucky day for building a house or starting a journey.
Ombiasy	A wise man who serves as a priest or magician of Madagascar's traditional tribal religions.
Pachypodium	A smooth-skinned, gourdlike plant that stores water in its hollow center and grows above ground, entirely without roots. It is found only in Madagascar.
Razana	The spirits of dead ancestors, who are believed to watch, protect, and advise the living.
Tanghena (also called *tanguin*)	A poison made from the oleander plant that was used for trial-by-ordeal during the reign of Queen Ranavalona the Terrible.
Traveler's tree	A tree whose thick, corklike trunk holds a liquid that can be drunk instead of water and

whose long, tough leaves are used to thatch roofs. The tree grows throughout Madagascar.

Vy Vato Sakelika (VVS)   A secret society formed in the early 1900s by Malagasy who believed that the island should be free of French rule. The VVS combined ancient Malagasy religious and magical rites with political activity.

Xerophytes   Plants that are specially adapted to survive drought and dry conditions. Many of the plants found in Madagascar's dry southern region are xerophytes.

Zebu   Cattle with large humps of fatty tissue behind their heads and long, curving horns. The Malagasy prize their zebu herds as signs of wealth.

Zoma   The central marketplace of Antananarivo, the island's capital. Its name comes from the Malagasy word for "Friday," because Friday used to be market day.

◀INDEX▶

ACKNOWLEDGMENTS
The author and publisher are grateful to the following sources for photographs: June Krupsaw Lenkin (pp. 36, 57, 58–64); Library of Congress (pp. 2, 16, 28, 30, 33, 34, 38, 40, 41, 43, 44, 46, 48, 51, 54, 66, 67, 72, 75, 76–77, 84, 87, 91, 96–97, 98, 100–101); National Archives (pp. 14, 20, 23, 25, 26, 69, 70, 85, 88); National Museum of African Art/ Eliot Elisofon Archives (p. 79); AP/Wide World Photos (pp. 53, 82); United Nations (p. 75); World Bank (pp. 18, 92–93, 94). Photo Editor: Marty Baldessari. Photo Research: Dixon & Turner Research Associates; Susan G. Holtz.